CONTAINER GARDENING
FOR BEGINNERS

A Step-by-Step Guide to Grow Your Own Vegetables, Fruits, and Herbs. The Simple, No-Fuss Way to Start Your Own Home Garden, Even with Limited Space or Experience.

Lewis Mercer

ISBN: 978-1-956289-24-4

Contents

Introduction

Why Grow Your Own Vegetables?

Growing your own vegetables is not only a rewarding activity but also a meaningful step toward healthier living. Home-grown produce is fresher, more flavorful, and often more nutritious than store-bought options. It allows you to control what goes into your food, including the absence of harmful chemicals, and promotes a deeper connection to what you eat. Whether you have a sprawling backyard, a modest balcony, or just a few windowsills, vegetable gardening opens the door to sustainable, local food production.

Benefits of Home Gardening

Health Benefits:

<u>Nutritional Value</u>: Freshly harvested vegetables are rich in vitamins, minerals, and antioxidants.

<u>Physical Activity</u>: Gardening keeps you active and reduces stress, contributing to mental and physical well-being.

<u>Mindfulness</u>: The process of planting and nurturing plants promotes mindfulness and relaxation.

Cost Savings:

Growing vegetables reduces grocery bills, especially when planting high-yield crops like lettuce, tomatoes, or beans. Savings extend to reducing trips to the store and reliance on packaged, processed foods.

Sustainability:

By growing your food, you minimize your carbon footprint and reliance on large-scale agriculture.

Composting kitchen scraps reduces waste and enriches your garden soil, creating a self-sustaining cycle.

Dispelling Myths: You Don't Need a Big Garden or Experience

Small Spaces Work: Even a windowsill or small balcony can produce herbs, leafy greens, or compact vegetables like cherry tomatoes.

Beginner-Friendly Options: Many vegetables, such as lettuce, radishes, and zucchini, are low-maintenance and forgiving, making them ideal for beginners.

Low-Cost Start: Starting a garden doesn't require expensive tools or fancy setups. With some soil, seeds, and water, you can get started almost anywhere.

By growing your own vegetables, you reap health benefits, save money, and contribute to a more sustainable future—all without needing extensive space or expertise. Gardening invites everyone to connect with nature, one seed at a time.

Getting Started

Starting your vegetable garden can seem like a daunting task, but it's easier than you think when you break it into manageable steps. The first thing to consider is where you'll grow your vegetables. The beauty of gardening is its flexibility— no matter how much or how little space you have, there's always a way to make it work. If you have a garden, you can dedicate a plot of land for planting. For those with limited outdoor areas, balconies and terraces offer excellent opportunities for container gardening, while windowsills can host smaller plants like herbs or compact vegetable varieties. The key is to choose a spot with enough sunlight, as most vegetables thrive with at least 6–8 hours of direct light daily.

Once you've identified your space, it's time to gather the essentials. You don't need an elaborate setup to start growing vegetables. A few basic items will suffice, such as pots or containers, which are vital for small spaces. These can range from classic terracotta pots to upcycled household items, as long as they have proper drainage. Soil is another crucial element, and for the best results, use nutrient-rich, well-draining soil tailored for vegetables. Simple tools like a trowel, hand fork, and watering can will make planting and maintenance easier. Fertilizers, either organic like compost or commercial, will ensure your plants have the nutrients they need to grow healthy and strong.

Budgeting for your first garden is important, but it doesn't have to break the bank. Many gardening beginners worry about costs, but starting small and expanding gradually can keep it affordable. Seeds are inexpensive and yield a lot, making them a cost-effective choice. For containers, repurposing old buckets or crates can save money, and compost can be made at home from kitchen scraps. With a modest initial investment, you'll soon find that growing your vegetables is not only economical but also deeply satisfying as you watch your efforts flourish.

By choosing the right space, equipping yourself with the basics, and planning within your budget, you'll be ready to embark on a fulfilling gardening journey that brings fresh, home-grown vegetables into your life.

Basic Equipment You'll Need

To start your vegetable gardening journey, having the right basic equipment is essential. While the tools of the trade might seem intimidating at first, you'll be surprised how simple and accessible it all is.

First, you'll need pots or containers, especially if you're gardening in small spaces like balconies, terraces, or windowsills. These can range from classic terracotta pots to upcycled items like buckets, crates, or even old tin cans. The key is ensuring they have proper drainage holes to prevent water from pooling at the bottom, which could harm plant roots.

Next comes soil, the foundation of any healthy garden. Choose a nutrient-rich, well-draining soil mix specifically designed for vegetables. If you're planting in the ground, enriching the existing soil with compost or organic matter will greatly improve its quality and fertility. Potting soil is ideal for container gardens, as it's lightweight and retains moisture without becoming waterlogged.

Tools are another essential component, though you don't need an extensive collection to get started. A trowel is indispensable for digging and planting, while a hand fork is perfect for loosening soil or removing weeds. For watering, a basic watering can with a gentle spray attachment will prevent splashing soil onto leaves, which can reduce the risk of disease. As your garden grows, you might find that a pair of gardening gloves and some pruning shears become handy additions to your toolkit.

Finally, consider fertilizers to give your vegetables the nutrients they need to thrive. Organic options like compost, manure, or worm castings are excellent for enriching the soil naturally. Commercial fertilizers are also available in slow-release granules or liquid form and can be tailored to specific plants, such as leafy greens or flowering vegetables.

By equipping yourself with these basic items, you'll have everything you need to create a thriving garden, no matter your space or experience level. As your confidence grows, you can gradually expand your toolkit and knowledge to explore new gardening challenges.

Understanding the Basics

Light, Water, and Soil: Key Factors for Healthy Plants

The foundation of a thriving garden lies in providing your plants with the right balance of light, water, and soil. These three elements work together to ensure healthy growth and productive harvests, no matter what you're growing.

Light is essential for photosynthesis, the process by which plants convert sunlight into energy. Most vegetables thrive in full sun, needing 6–8 hours of direct sunlight daily. If you're gardening in a shaded area, focus on plants that tolerate less light, such as lettuce, spinach, or herbs like mint. Observe your garden space throughout the day to determine where sunlight falls, and plan your planting accordingly. For indoor gardening, consider using grow lights to provide the necessary spectrum of light.

Water is the lifeblood of plants, and proper hydration is crucial. While plants differ in their water needs, most vegetables prefer consistently moist soil. Overwatering, however, can lead to root rot and other issues, so it's important to strike the right balance. Check the soil's moisture by inserting your finger an inch or two deep; if it feels dry, it's time to water. Early morning is the best time to water, as it minimizes evaporation and allows plants to absorb moisture before the heat of the day. For container gardening, ensure pots have proper drainage to prevent waterlogging.

Soil provides nutrients and stability for plant roots, acting as the foundation for healthy growth. The ideal soil is rich in organic matter, well-draining, and slightly loose to allow roots to grow easily. Testing your soil's pH and nutrient levels can help you tailor it to your plants' needs. Most vegetables prefer a slightly acidic to neutral pH (6–7). Adding compost or aged manure enriches the soil, while mulching helps retain moisture and suppress weeds. For container gardens, choose high-quality potting soil specifically designed for vegetables.

By understanding and managing these three key factors, you create an environment where plants can thrive. With a little observation and care, your garden will flourish, providing fresh, healthy produce throughout the growing season.

Seasonal Planting

What to Grow and When

The success of your vegetable garden largely depends on timing. Each season brings unique opportunities for planting, as different crops thrive in varying conditions. By understanding what to grow and when, you can plan a productive garden year-round.

Spring: The Season of Growth

Spring marks the beginning of the gardening year, offering cool temperatures and ample rainfall—perfect for starting many crops. As soon as the soil is workable, plant cool-season vegetables like lettuce, spinach, radishes, and peas. These crops thrive in the mild temperatures of early spring and can be sown directly into the ground or in containers. As the season progresses and temperatures warm, you can transplant seedlings of broccoli, cabbage, and kale, as well as begin sowing heat-loving crops like tomatoes, peppers, and cucumbers indoors to prepare for summer planting.

Summer: Peak Productivity

Summer is the time for abundant growth and harvesting. Warm-season vegetables like tomatoes, zucchini, beans, and corn flourish in the long, sunny days. Succession planting ensures continuous harvests—once early crops like radishes or lettuce are harvested, replace them with quick-growing summer vegetables. Regular watering and mulching are essential during this season to protect plants from heat stress and to retain soil moisture. Herbs like basil and cilantro also thrive in summer, providing fresh flavors for seasonal cooking.

Fall: Preparing for Cooler Days

As summer winds down, fall offers another opportunity to grow. Cooler temperatures make it ideal for planting a second round of leafy greens, carrots, and beets. Hardy vegetables like Brussels sprouts and cauliflower can be transplanted into the garden, as they grow well in the cooler months and even taste sweeter after a light frost. To extend your growing season, use row covers or cold frames to protect plants from early frosts.

Winter: Planning and Preservation

Winter may seem like a dormant period, but it's a crucial time for planning and preparation. In milder climates, hardy crops like kale, spinach, and garlic can continue to grow, provided they are protected with mulch or row covers. Indoors, herbs like parsley and chives can thrive on sunny windowsills. Use this time to plan next season's garden, order seeds, and prepare your soil by adding compost or organic matter.

Timing is Everything

By understanding seasonal cycles and your local climate, you can optimize your planting schedule to keep your garden productive throughout the year. A well-timed garden not only maximizes harvests but also ensures that you're always enjoying fresh, seasonal produce. With careful planning and attention to seasonal rhythms, your garden can thrive no matter the time of year.

Common Mistake to Avoid

Common Mistakes to Avoid

Embarking on your gardening journey can be exciting and rewarding, but it's easy to make mistakes along the way. Understanding common pitfalls will help you avoid them and set your plants up for success.

1. Planting at the Wrong Time

Timing is crucial in gardening. Planting too early, especially in cold soil, can stunt growth or kill seeds and seedlings. On the other hand, planting too late may not give crops enough time to mature. Always check the recommended planting times for your region and specific plants, considering frost dates and seasonal temperatures.

2. Overwatering or Underwatering

Watering issues are among the most frequent causes of plant stress. Overwatering can lead to root rot, while underwatering causes wilting and slow growth. Plants need consistently moist—but not soggy—soil. Check soil moisture by touching it; water when it feels dry an inch below the surface, and adjust for weather conditions.

3. Poor Soil Preparation

Skipping soil preparation is a recipe for poor plant health. Neglecting to test soil pH, add compost, or address drainage issues can lead to nutrient deficiencies and stunted growth. Take time to enrich your soil with organic matter and test its suitability for the crops you want to grow.

4. Overcrowding Plants

It can be tempting to plant densely to maximize space, but overcrowding reduces airflow, increases competition for nutrients, and encourages disease. Follow spacing guidelines for each plant to ensure they have room to grow and thrive.

5. Ignoring Sunlight Requirements

Different plants have different light needs. Placing a full-sun plant in a shady spot will lead to weak, leggy growth and poor yields. Conversely, shade-loving plants placed in direct sun may scorch. Observe your garden to determine sun patterns and match plants to their preferred light conditions.

6. Neglecting Weeds

Weeds compete with your vegetables for water, nutrients, and sunlight. If left unchecked, they can quickly overtake your garden. Regular weeding or using mulch to suppress weed growth is essential to maintaining healthy plants.

7. Skipping Crop Rotation

Planting the same crops in the same spot year after year depletes the soil of specific nutrients and encourages pests and diseases. Rotate crops annually to maintain soil health and disrupt pest cycles.

8. Over-Fertilizing

While it's important to feed your plants, using too much fertilizer can do more harm than good, leading to excessive foliage growth at the expense of fruit or root development. Use fertilizers sparingly and follow the recommendations for your specific crops.

9. Neglecting Pests and Diseases

Ignoring the early signs of pests or diseases can result in widespread damage. Regularly inspect your plants for issues and act promptly to manage problems using natural or chemical methods.

10. Expecting Instant Results

Gardening requires patience. Plants take time to grow, mature, and bear fruit. Expecting immediate results can lead to frustration. Instead, embrace the process and learn from each growing season.

By avoiding these common mistakes, you'll set yourself up for a more successful and enjoyable gardening experience. Remember, every gardener learns through trial and error, so approach challenges as opportunities to grow alongside your plants!

Plant Profiles

Basil

Basil is an aromatic herb widely used in Italian and Mediterranean cuisines for sauces, salads, and garnishes.

Difficulty Level: Very easy, suitable for beginners.

Characteristics

Life Cycle: Annual.

Size: Grows to a height of 12–24 inches (30–60 cm).

Ideal Conditions

Light: Prefers full sunlight (6–8 hours daily).

Climate: Thrives in warm climates; sensitive to frost.

Space: Suitable for pots 8 inches (20 cm) in diameter or garden beds.

Preparation

Soil: Well-drained, nutrient-rich, with pH 6–7.5.

Pot/Vessel: Minimum depth of 6–8 inches (15–20 cm).

Initial Fertilization: Add compost or organic fertilizer before planting.

Planting

Timing: Plant in spring when the risk of frost has passed (March–May, depending on the region).

Method:

From Seed: Sow seeds 1/4 inch (0.6 cm) deep and 2 inches (5 cm) apart. Thin to 6–12 inches (15–30 cm) once seedlings sprout.

From Seedlings: Transplant when seedlings have 2–3 sets of leaves. Space 12 inches (30 cm) apart.

Germination: Seeds germinate in 7–14 days.

Daily Care

Watering: Moderate; keep soil moist but not waterlogged.

Fertilizing: Apply a balanced, organic fertilizer every 2–3 weeks.

Pruning: Regularly pinch off flowers and prune leaves to encourage growth.

Pest and Disease Management

Common Issues:

Aphids or whiteflies.

Fungal diseases such as powdery mildew.

Solutions: Use neem oil or garlic spray for pests. Ensure good air circulation to prevent diseases.

Harvesting

When: 6–8 weeks after planting, once the plant is about 6 inches (15 cm) tall.

How: Pick leaves as needed, starting from the top to encourage further growth.

Practical Tips

Companion Planting: Grow basil near tomatoes and peppers to deter pests.

Propagation: Can also be propagated by placing cuttings in water.

Curiosities

Historically regarded as a symbol of love and protection in many cultures.

Parsley

Parsley is a versatile herb used for garnishing and flavoring dishes in cuisines worldwide.

Difficulty Level: Easy, suitable for beginners.

Characteristics

Life Cycle: Biennial (treated as annual for continuous harvest).

Size: Grows to 12–18 inches (30–45 cm) tall.

Ideal Conditions

Light: Prefers full sun but tolerates partial shade.

Climate: Thrives in moderate climates; sensitive to extreme heat and frost.

Space: Suitable for pots 8 inches (20 cm) in diameter or directly in garden beds.

Preparation

Soil: Rich, well-draining soil with pH 6-7.

Pot/Vessel: Minimum depth of 8-10 inches (20–25 cm).

Initial Fertilization: Use compost or an organic fertilizer before planting.

Planting

Indoors: Start seeds 6–8 weeks before the last frost date.

Outdoors: Plant seeds or seedlings in spring after frost risk has passed (March–May).

Method:

From Seed: Soak seeds in warm water for 24 hours before sowing. Plant seeds 1/4 inch (0.6 cm) deep and 6–8 inches (15–20 cm) apart.

From Seedlings: Transplant when seedlings have at least 3 sets of leaves. Space 6–10 inches (15–25 cm) apart.

Germination: Seeds germinate slowly, typically in 14–28 days

Daily Care

Watering: Keep soil consistently moist but not waterlogged.

Fertilizing: Apply a balanced fertilizer every 4–6 weeks for optimal growth.

Pruning: Remove yellow or dead leaves regularly.

Pest and Disease Management

Common Issues:

Aphids and caterpillars.

Fungal diseases like leaf spot.

Solutions: Spray neem oil for pests; avoid overhead watering to prevent fungal growth.

Harvesting

When: Ready for harvest 70–90 days after sowing.

How: Cut stems from the base, starting with the outermost leaves, leaving the inner growth to continue producing.

Practical Tips

Companion Planting: Grows well with tomatoes, carrots, and asparagus. Avoid planting near mint.

Propagation: Propagate by seeds or dividing older plants.

Curiosities

Parsley is rich in vitamins A, C, and K and has been used historically for medicinal purposes, including digestion and breath freshening.

Mint

Mint is a fragrant herb used in teas, beverages, desserts, and savory dishes. It is also known for its medicinal properties.

Difficulty Level: Very easy, but requires containment to prevent spreading.

Characteristics

Life Cycle: Perennial.

Size: Grows 12–24 inches (30–60 cm) tall, spreads aggressively via underground runners.

Ideal Conditions

Light: Prefers partial shade to full sun.

Climate: Thrives in moderate climates but tolerates a wide range of conditions.

Space: Grows well in containers or confined garden areas to limit spreading.

Preparation

Soil: Rich, moist, well-draining soil with pH 6–7.

Pot/Vessel: Minimum depth of 8–12 inches (20–30 cm), with adequate drainage.

Initial Fertilization: Mix compost or organic fertilizer into the soil before planting.

Planting

Plant in spring (March–May) when the soil is warm.

Method:

From Cuttings: Place cuttings in water until roots form, then plant directly into the soil.

From Seedlings: Transplant seedlings into pots or garden beds, spacing 12–18 inches (30–45 cm) apart.

From Seeds: Sow seeds 1/4 inch (0.6 cm) deep; germination takes 10–15 days.

Daily Care

Watering: Keep soil consistently moist but not waterlogged.

Fertilizing: Apply a balanced fertilizer every 6–8 weeks or topdress with compost.

Pruning: Regularly pinch back stems to encourage bushy growth and prevent flowering.

Pest and Disease Management

Common Issues:

Aphids, spider mites, and whiteflies.

Rust and powdery mildew in damp conditions.

Solutions: Use neem oil for pests and ensure good air circulation to prevent fungal issues.

Harvesting

When: Begin harvesting once the plant reaches 4–6 inches (10–15 cm) tall.

How: Pinch off leaves or cut stems, leaving at least 1/3 of the plant to regrow.

Practical Tips

Companion Planting: Grows well with cabbage, tomatoes, and carrots but avoid planting near parsley.

Propagation: Easily propagated from stem cuttings or by dividing the root ball.

Curiosities

Mint varieties include spearmint, peppermint, and chocolate mint, each with distinct flavors.

Historically, mint was a symbol of hospitality and was used to freshen air and clean tables.

Rosemary

Rosemary is a fragrant, woody herb used in cooking, aromatherapy, and as a decorative shrub in gardens.

Difficulty Level: Easy to grow; thrives with minimal maintenance.

Characteristics

Life Cycle: Perennial.

Size: Grows 2–4 feet (60–120 cm) tall and wide, depending on the variety.

Ideal Conditions

Light: Full sun (6–8 hours daily).

Climate: Prefers warm, dry climates; tolerates light frost but not extreme cold.

Space: Suitable for garden beds or containers with a minimum depth of 12 inches (30 cm).

Preparation

Soil: Well-drained, sandy or loamy soil with pH 6–7. Avoid heavy clay soils.

Pot/Vessel: Use a pot with good drainage, at least 12 inches (30 cm) in diameter.

Initial Fertilization: Mix organic compost or a slow-release fertilizer into the soil before planting.

Planting

Outdoors: Plant in spring (March–May) after the last frost.

Indoors: Can be started any time of year in a sunny window.

Method:

From Seeds: Sow seeds 1/4 inch (0.6 cm) deep in trays; transplant when seedlings are 2–3 inches (5–8 cm) tall. Germination can take 2–4 weeks.

From Cuttings: Propagate by placing 4–6 inch (10–15 cm) cuttings in water until roots form, then plant directly into the soil.

From Seedlings: Transplant into garden beds or pots, spacing 18–24 inches (45–60 cm) apart.

Daily Care

Watering: Allow the soil to dry out between waterings. Rosemary prefers dry conditions over waterlogging.

Fertilizing: Feed with a balanced fertilizer once a month during the growing season or use compost as a topdressing.

Pruning: Trim regularly to maintain shape and promote growth. Avoid heavy pruning in late fall to prevent damage.

Pest and Disease Management

Common Issues:

Aphids, spider mites, and whiteflies.

Root rot in poorly drained soil.

Solutions: Use neem oil for pests; ensure soil drains well to prevent root rot.

Harvesting

When: Begin harvesting once the plant is well established, typically 6–12 months after planting.

How: Snip off sprigs as needed, ideally before flowering for the most flavorful leaves.

Practical Tips

Companion Planting: Grows well with sage, thyme, and lavender. Avoid planting near overly thirsty plants.

Winter Protection: In colder climates, bring potted rosemary indoors during winter or cover outdoor plants with frost protection.

Curiosities

Rosemary has been associated with memory and fidelity since ancient times and was used in weddings and funerals as a symbol of remembrance.

Lettuce

Lettuce is a cool-season leafy vegetable enjoyed in salads, sandwiches, and wraps. It comes in various types, including romaine, butterhead, iceberg, and loose-leaf.

Difficulty Level: Very easy, ideal for beginners.

Characteristics

Life Cycle: Annual.

Size: Height ranges from 6–12 inches (15–30 cm), depending on the variety.

Ideal Conditions

Light: Prefers full sun in cool climates; partial shade in warmer regions.

Climate: Thrives in cool temperatures, 60–70°F (15–21°C). Heat can cause bolting (premature flowering).

Space: Grows well in garden beds or shallow containers at least 6 inches (15 cm) deep.

Preparation

Soil: Loose, well-draining, nutrient-rich soil with pH 6–6.8.

Pot/Vessel: Minimum depth of 6–8 inches (15–20 cm).

Initial Fertilization: Add compost or a balanced organic fertilizer before planting.

Planting

Timing:

Spring: Start indoors or outdoors 2–4 weeks before the last frost date.

Fall: Plant 6–8 weeks before the first expected frost.

For continuous harvest: Sow seeds every 2 weeks.

Method:

From Seeds: Sow seeds 1/4 inch (0.6 cm) deep and 6–12 inches (15–30 cm) apart, depending on the variety.

From Transplants: Space plants 6–12 inches (15–30 cm) apart, ensuring enough room for growth.

Germination: Seeds germinate in 7–10 days at 50–75°F (10–24°C).

Daily Care

Watering: Keep soil evenly moist but not waterlogged. Lettuce has shallow roots and requires consistent watering.

Fertilizing: Apply a diluted liquid fertilizer every 2–3 weeks, especially for leaf varieties.

Weeding: Keep the area weed-free to avoid competition for nutrients and moisture.

Pest and Disease Management

Common Issues:

Aphids, slugs, and caterpillars.

Fungal diseases like downy mildew.

Solutions: Use neem oil for pests and ensure good air circulation to prevent diseases. Use organic slug traps or diatomaceous earth for slug control.

Harvesting

When: Ready to harvest 30–70 days after planting, depending on the variety.

How:

Leaf Lettuce: Harvest outer leaves as needed, leaving the inner leaves to continue growing.

Head Lettuce: Cut the entire head at the base when fully formed.

Practical Tips

Companion Planting: Grows well with carrots, radishes, and onions. Avoid planting near broccoli or cabbage.

Bolting Prevention: Provide shade during hot weather and mulch to keep soil cool.

Curiosities

Lettuce was cultivated over 4,500 years ago in Egypt and was considered sacred, symbolizing health and prosperity.

Arugula

Arugula is a fast-growing, peppery-flavored leafy green used in salads, sandwiches, and pasta dishes. It is also known as rocket or rucola.

Difficulty Level: Very easy, suitable for beginners.

Characteristics

Life Cycle: Annual (sometimes grown as a short-lived perennial in mild climates).

Size: Grows 6–12 inches (15–30 cm) tall.

Ideal Conditions

Light: Prefers full sun but tolerates partial shade, especially in warmer climates.

Climate: Thrives in cool temperatures, 45–65°F (7–18°C). Hot weather can cause bolting (premature flowering).

Space: Grows well in garden beds or containers at least 6 inches (15 cm) deep.

Preparation

Soil: Well-draining, fertile soil with a slightly acidic to neutral pH of 6–7.

Pot/Vessel: Minimum depth of 6–8 inches (15–20 cm).

Initial Fertilization: Mix compost or a balanced organic fertilizer into the soil before planting.

Planting

Timing:

Spring: Plant 2–4 weeks before the last frost date.

Fall: Sow seeds 4–6 weeks before the first frost.

For continuous harvest: Sow seeds every 2–3 weeks.

Method:

From Seeds: Sow seeds 1/4 inch (0.6 cm) deep, spacing 1 inch (2.5 cm) apart in rows 6–12 inches (15–30 cm) apart.

From Transplants: Space 4–6 inches (10–15 cm) apart for individual plants.

Germination: Seeds germinate in 5–7 days at 40–75°F (4–24°C).

Daily Care

Watering: Keep soil consistently moist but not waterlogged.

Fertilizing: Apply a light, balanced fertilizer once during the growing season if soil fertility is low.

Weeding: Keep the area weed-free to avoid competition for nutrients and moisture.

Pest and Disease Management

Common Issues:

Flea beetles and aphids.

Downy mildew and powdery mildew in damp conditions.

Solutions: Use neem oil for pests and ensure good air circulation to prevent fungal diseases. Row covers can protect young plants from flea beetles.

Harvesting

When: Ready to harvest 20–40 days after planting.

How:

Baby Leaves: Harvest when leaves are 2–3 inches (5–7 cm) long.

Mature Leaves: Cut the outer leaves first, allowing the inner ones to continue growing.

Whole Plant: Cut at the base when the plant matures, especially before bolting.

Practical Tips

Companion Planting: Grows well with carrots, radishes, and lettuce. Avoid planting near crops in the cabbage family to reduce pest risks.

Bolting Prevention: In hot climates, grow arugula in partial shade and keep the soil cool with mulch.

Curiosities

Arugula has been a favorite in Mediterranean cuisine for centuries and was considered an aphrodisiac in ancient Rome.

Spinach

Spinach is a nutrient-rich leafy green popular in salads, smoothies, and cooked dishes. It grows quickly and thrives in cool weather.

Difficulty Level: Easy to grow; suitable for beginners.

Characteristics

Life Cycle: Annual.

Size: Grows 6–12 inches (15–30 cm) tall, depending on the variety.

Ideal Conditions

Light: Prefers full sun to partial shade.

Climate: Thrives in cool weather, 50–70°F (10–21°C). High heat causes bolting (premature flowering).

Space: Grows well in garden beds or containers with at least 6 inches (15 cm) depth.

Preparation

Soil: Rich, well-draining soil with a pH of 6–7.5.

Pot/Vessel: Minimum depth of 6–8 inches (15–20 cm).

Initial Fertilization: Mix compost or a balanced organic fertilizer into the soil before planting.

Planting

Timing:

Spring: Plant 4–6 weeks before the last frost.

Fall: Sow 6–8 weeks before the first frost.

For continuous harvest: Sow seeds every 2–3 weeks during the growing season.

Method:

From Seeds: Sow seeds 1/2 inch (1.2 cm) deep and 1–2 inches (2.5–5 cm) apart. Thin seedlings to 3–6 inches (8–15 cm) apart once they sprout.

From Transplants: Space plants 3–6 inches (8–15 cm) apart.

Germination: Seeds germinate in 5–10 days at 45–75°F (7–24°C).

Daily Care

Watering: Keep the soil consistently moist but not waterlogged. Spinach has shallow roots and requires regular watering.

Fertilizing: Apply a nitrogen-rich fertilizer every 2–3 weeks to encourage leafy growth.

Weeding: Remove weeds to prevent competition for nutrients and water.

Pest and Disease Management

Common Issues:

Leaf miners, aphids, and slugs.

Downy mildew and fungal leaf spots.

Solutions: Use neem oil or insecticidal soap for pests, and ensure proper spacing and airflow to reduce disease risk.

Harvesting

When: Ready to harvest 30–45 days after planting.

How:

Baby Leaves: Harvest when leaves are 2–3 inches (5–7 cm) long.

Mature Leaves: Pick outer leaves first, allowing the inner leaves to grow.

Whole Plant: Cut at the base if harvesting all at once.

Practical Tips

Companion Planting: Grows well with radishes, carrots, and onions. Avoid planting near potatoes.

Bolting Prevention: In warm climates, provide partial shade and keep the soil cool with mulch.

Curiosities

Spinach is native to Persia and has been cultivated for over 2,000 years. It's famous for its high iron and vitamin content, though its iron absorption rate is moderated by oxalates.

Kale

Kale is a nutrient-rich leafy green known for its hardiness and versatility in salads, smoothies, soups, and chips.

Difficulty Level: Easy, ideal for beginners and resilient to various conditions.

Characteristics

Life Cycle: Biennial (commonly grown as an annual).

Size: Grows 12–24 inches (30–60 cm) tall, depending on the variety.

Ideal Conditions

Light: Prefers full sun but tolerates partial shade.

Climate: Thrives in cool weather, 40–75°F (4–24°C). Becomes sweeter after a light frost.

Space: Grows well in garden beds or containers with a depth of at least 12 inches (30 cm).

Preparation

Soil: Rich, well-draining soil with a pH of 6–7.

Pot/Vessel: Minimum depth of 12 inches (30 cm).

Initial Fertilization: Mix compost or a nitrogen-rich organic fertilizer into the soil before planting.

Planting

Timing:

Spring: Start seeds indoors 6–8 weeks before the last frost or sow directly outdoors 2–4 weeks before the last frost.

Fall: Sow seeds 6–8 weeks before the first frost for a fall/winter harvest.

Method:

From Seeds: Sow seeds 1/4–1/2 inch (0.6–1.2 cm) deep and 1 inch (2.5 cm) apart in rows 12–18 inches (30–45 cm) apart. Thin to 12–18 inches (30–45 cm) apart once seedlings emerge.

From Transplants: Space seedlings 12–18 inches (30–45 cm) apart.

Germination: Seeds germinate in 5–10 days at 45–85°F (7–29°C).

Daily Care

Watering: Keep soil evenly moist but not waterlogged; kale needs about 1–1.5 inches (2.5–4 cm) of water per week.

Fertilizing: Feed with a nitrogen-rich fertilizer every 3–4 weeks for optimal leaf production.

Weeding: Keep the area weed-free to avoid competition for nutrients and water.

Pest and Disease Management

Common Issues:

Aphids, cabbage worms, and flea beetles.

Fungal diseases like powdery mildew.

Solutions: Use neem oil or insecticidal soap for pests and practice crop rotation to reduce disease risk. Cover plants with row covers to prevent pests.

Harvesting

When: Ready to harvest 50–75 days after planting.

How:

Young Leaves: Begin harvesting once leaves are 4–6 inches (10–15 cm) long.

Mature Leaves: Pick the outermost leaves first, leaving the central bud to continue growing.

Whole Plant: Cut at the base if harvesting all at once.

Practical Tips

Companion Planting: Grows well with beets, celery, and onions. Avoid planting near tomatoes or beans.

Frost Sweetening: Kale leaves become sweeter after exposure to light frosts, making fall and winter harvests particularly flavorful.

Curiosities

Kale has been cultivated for over 2,000 years and was a staple crop in ancient Rome. It is renowned for its high vitamin K, C, and iron content.

Cherry Tomatoes

Cherry tomatoes are small, sweet, and juicy fruits ideal for salads, snacking, or cooking. They grow prolifically and are suitable for container gardening

Difficulty Level: Easy, but requires regular care.

Characteristics

Life Cycle: Annual.

Size: Plants grow 2–6 feet (60–180 cm) tall, depending on the variety.

Types: Determinate (bush type) and indeterminate (vine type, continues to grow and produce fruit).

Ideal Conditions

Light: Full sun (6–8 hours daily).

Climate: Warm and frost-free, 70–85°F (21–29°C) is ideal for fruiting.

Space: Suitable for containers (minimum 5-gallon pot) or garden beds.

Preparation

Soil: Well-draining, nutrient-rich soil with pH 6–7.

Pot/Vessel: Minimum depth of 12–18 inches (30–45 cm).

Initial Fertilization: Incorporate compost or a balanced organic fertilizer into the soil before planting.

Planting

Timing:

Indoors: Start seeds 6–8 weeks before the last frost.

Outdoors: Transplant seedlings 2–3 weeks after the last frost when nighttime temperatures stay above 50°F (10°C).

Method:

From Seeds: Sow seeds 1/4 inch (0.6 cm) deep in seed trays or small pots.

From Transplants: Plant seedlings deeply, burying the stem up to the first set of true leaves to encourage a strong root system.

Spacing:

Garden: Space plants 24–36 inches (60–90 cm) apart.

Containers: One plant per pot.

Daily Care

Watering: Keep the soil evenly moist but not waterlogged; water deeply 1–2 times per week.

Fertilizing: Apply a balanced fertilizer (e.g., 10-10-10) every 2–3 weeks, or use a tomato-specific fertilizer.

Staking/Support:

Indeterminate: Use cages, stakes, or trellises to support growth.

Determinate: May require light staking.

Pruning: Remove suckers (small shoots between the main stem and branches) for indeterminate varieties to improve airflow and fruit production.

Pest and Disease Management

Common Issues:

Aphids, whiteflies, and hornworms.

Diseases like blight and blossom-end rot.

Solutions: Use neem oil or insecticidal soap for pests. Avoid overwatering and maintain consistent soil moisture to prevent rot.

Harvesting

When: Cherry tomatoes are ready to harvest 60–75 days after planting.

How:

Pick when fruits are fully colored and slightly firm.

Gently twist or snip fruits from the vine to avoid damaging the plant.

Practical Tips

Companion Planting: Grow near basil, marigolds, and carrots to repel pests. Avoid planting near corn or potatoes.

Mulching: Add a layer of mulch to retain soil moisture and prevent weeds.

Continuous Production: Indeterminate varieties will produce fruit all season; determinate types will yield in a shorter period.

Curiosities

Cherry tomatoes originate from South America and were cultivated by the Aztecs. They're prized for their high antioxidants, especially lycopene.

Peppers (Bell and Chili)

Peppers are warm-season crops, ranging from sweet bell peppers to spicy chili varieties, used in cooking and fresh dishes.

Difficulty Level: Moderate, requiring warm temperatures and consistent care.

Characteristics

Life Cycle: Annual in most climates (perennial in tropical zones).

Size: Plants grow 18–36 inches (45–90 cm) tall, depending on the variety.

Ideal Conditions

Light: Full sun (6–8 hours daily).

Climate: Warm temperatures, 70–85°F (21–29°C). Peppers are frost-sensitive and thrive in consistent warmth.

Space: Suitable for containers (at least 12 inches/30 cm deep) or garden beds.

Preparation

Soil: Well-draining, fertile soil with pH 6–7.

Pot/Vessel: Use a container with good drainage, at least 3 gallons for each plant.

Initial Fertilization: Enrich soil with compost or a balanced fertilizer before planting.

Planting

Indoors: Start seeds 8–10 weeks before the last frost date.

Outdoors: Transplant 2–3 weeks after the last frost when nighttime temperatures remain above 55°F (13°C).

Method:

From Seeds: Sow seeds 1/4 inch (0.6 cm) deep in seed trays or small pots.

From Transplants: Plant seedlings slightly deeper than their original container depth.

Spacing:

Garden: Space plants 12–18 inches (30–45 cm) apart in rows spaced 24–36 inches (60–90 cm) apart.

Containers: One plant per container.

Daily Care

Watering: Water regularly to keep soil evenly moist but not waterlogged; 1–2 inches (2.5–5 cm) of water per week.

Fertilizing:

Apply a low-nitrogen, high-phosphorus fertilizer (e.g., 5-10-10) when flowers appear to support fruiting.

Use compost tea or a balanced liquid fertilizer every 2–3 weeks during the growing season.

Support: Provide stakes or cages to support plants as they grow and produce heavy fruit.

Mulching: Add a 2–3 inch (5–7.5 cm) layer of mulch to retain soil moisture and suppress weeds.

Pest and Disease Management

Common Issues:

Aphids, whiteflies, and spider mites.

Fungal diseases such as blight and bacterial leaf spot.

Solutions: Use neem oil or insecticidal soap for pests. Avoid overhead watering and ensure good airflow to prevent diseases.

Harvesting

When:

Bell Peppers: Ready to harvest 60–90 days after transplanting, depending on the variety.

Chili Peppers: Harvested green or red (or other mature colors), typically 70–100 days after transplanting.

How:

Use scissors or pruning shears to cut fruit from the plant to avoid damaging stems.

For a spicier taste, allow chili peppers to ripen fully on the plant.

Practical Tips

Companion Planting: Grow with basil, onions, or carrots to deter pests. Avoid planting near fennel or beans.

Temperature Sensitivity: Peppers are sensitive to temperature extremes; use row covers during cold nights and shade during excessive heat.

Pollination: Shake plants gently or use a soft brush to improve pollination for more fruit.

Curiosities

Peppers originate from Central and South America. Capsaicin, the compound responsible for the spiciness in chili peppers, is concentrated in the seeds and white membranes.

Zucchini

Zucchini is a fast-growing summer squash prized for its mild flavor and versatility in cooking. It produces prolifically with proper care

Difficulty Level: Easy to grow, ideal for beginners.

Characteristics

Life Cycle: Annual.

Size: Plants can grow 2–3 feet (60–90 cm) wide and 1–3 feet (30–90 cm) tall, with vining or bush habits depending on the variety.

Ideal Conditions

Light: Full sun (6–8 hours daily).

Climate: Warm weather, 65–85°F (18–29°C). Sensitive to frost and extreme heat.

Space: Suitable for garden beds or large containers (at least 18 inches/45 cm wide).

Preparation

Soil: Rich, well-draining soil with pH 6–7.5.

Pot/Vessel: Minimum depth of 12–18 inches (30–45 cm).

Initial Fertilization: Mix compost or a balanced organic fertilizer into the soil before planting.

Planting

Timing:

Direct Sow: Plant seeds outdoors after the last frost when soil temperature is at least 60°F (16°C).

Transplanting: Start seeds indoors 3–4 weeks before the last frost and transplant outdoors after the last frost.

Method:

From Seeds: Sow seeds 1 inch (2.5 cm) deep, spacing 2–3 seeds together. Thin to 1 plant per space after germination.

From Transplants: Plant seedlings with 1–2 sets of true leaves, spacing them adequately.

Spacing:

Bush Varieties: Space plants 24–36 inches (60–90 cm) apart.

Vining Varieties: Allow 36–48 inches (90–120 cm) between plants or use a trellis to save space.

Germination: Seeds germinate in 5–10 days at 70–95°F (21–35°C).

Daily Care

Watering: Water deeply 1–2 times a week, keeping the soil consistently moist but not waterlogged.

Fertilizing:

Apply a balanced fertilizer (e.g., 10-10-10) every 4 weeks.

Use compost tea or diluted liquid fertilizer during flowering and fruiting stages.

Mulching: Use a 2–3 inch (5–7.5 cm) layer of mulch to retain soil moisture and suppress weeds.

Pollination: Ensure pollination by encouraging bees with companion flowers or hand-pollinate using a small brush.

Pest and Disease Management

Common Issues:

Pests: Squash bugs, cucumber beetles, and vine borers.

Diseases: Powdery mildew and blossom-end rot.

Solutions:

Use row covers for young plants to protect against pests.

Apply neem oil for pest control and ensure proper spacing and airflow to prevent fungal diseases.

Harvesting

When: Ready to harvest 40–55 days after planting.

How:

Pick fruits when they are 6–8 inches (15–20 cm) long for the best texture and flavor.

Use scissors or pruning shears to cut zucchinis from the plant, leaving a small stem attached.

Practical Tips

Companion Planting: Grow near beans, corn, or marigolds. Avoid planting near potatoes.

Continuous Harvesting: Regularly picking zucchini encourages the plant to produce more fruit.

Overripe Fruit: Large zucchinis can be used for baking (e.g., zucchini bread).

Curiosities

Zucchini is native to the Americas and was cultivated by Indigenous peoples for centuries. Its flowers are edible and often used in gourmet dishes.

Cucumbers

Cucumbers are a refreshing and crunchy fruit used in salads, pickling, and as snacks. They grow as vines or compact bush varieties

Difficulty Level: Moderate, requiring warm conditions and consistent care.

Characteristics

Life Cycle: Annual.

Size: Vining types can grow 6–8 feet (1.8–2.4 m) long; bush types remain compact, about 2–3 feet (60–90 cm) wide.

Ideal Conditions

Light: Full sun (6–8 hours daily).

Climate: Warm temperatures, 70–90°F (21–32°C). Sensitive to frost and cold soil.

Space: Grows well in garden beds, raised beds, or large containers (12 inches/30 cm deep).

Preparation

Soil: Fertile, well-draining soil with a pH of 6–7.

Pot/Vessel: Minimum depth of 12–18 inches (30–45 cm), with drainage holes.

Initial Fertilization: Incorporate compost or a balanced organic fertilizer before planting.

Planting

Timing:

Direct Sow: Plant seeds outdoors after the last frost when soil temperature is at least 60°F (16°C).

Transplanting: Start seeds indoors 3–4 weeks before the last frost and transplant after the soil warms.

Method:

From Seeds: Sow seeds 1/2 inch (1.3 cm) deep and 6 inches (15 cm) apart. Thin seedlings to the recommended spacing once they sprout.

From Transplants: Plant seedlings 6–8 inches (15–20 cm) apart for bush types or 12 inches (30 cm) apart for vining types.

Spacing:

Vining Types: Provide 36–48 inches (90–120 cm) between rows or use a trellis to save space.

Bush Types: Space plants 18–24 inches (45–60 cm) apart.

Germination: Seeds germinate in 3–10 days at 70–85°F (21–29°C).

Daily Care

Watering: Keep soil evenly moist, watering deeply 1–2 times per week to prevent bitterness in cucumbers.

Fertilizing:

Apply a balanced fertilizer every 2–3 weeks.

During flowering and fruiting, switch to a fertilizer high in potassium and phosphorus.

Mulching: Use mulch to retain soil moisture, regulate temperature, and prevent weeds.

Trellising: Use a trellis or support for vining varieties to save space and promote airflow.

Pest and Disease Management

Common Issues:

Pests: Cucumber beetles, aphids, and spider mites.

Diseases: Powdery mildew, downy mildew, and bacterial wilt.

Solutions:

Use neem oil or insecticidal soap for pest control.

Ensure proper spacing and airflow to prevent fungal diseases. Rotate crops yearly to reduce disease buildup.

Harvesting

When: Ready to harvest 50–70 days after planting, depending on the variety.

How:

Pick cucumbers when they are firm, green, and 6–8 inches (15–20 cm) long for slicing types.

For pickling cucumbers, harvest when 2–4 inches (5–10 cm) long.

Use scissors or a knife to cut the fruit from the vine to avoid damaging the plant.

Practical Tips

Companion Planting: Grows well with beans, corn, and radishes. Avoid planting near potatoes.

Pollination: Encourage pollinators by planting flowers nearby. For indoor or greenhouse plants, hand-pollinate using a small brush.

Curiosities: *Cucumbers originated in South Asia and were cultivated over 3,000 years ago. They are 95% water, making them a hydrating and refreshing snack.*

Radish

Radishes are fast-growing root vegetables, popular for their crisp texture and peppery flavor, perfect for salads and garnishes

Difficulty Level: Very easy, ideal for beginners.

Characteristics

Life Cycle: Annual.

Size: Grows 4–6 inches (10–15 cm) tall with roots 1–4 inches (2.5–10 cm) long, depending on the variety.

Ideal Conditions

Light: Full sun to partial shade.

Climate: Thrives in cool weather, 50–70°F (10–21°C). Warmer temperatures can cause spicier radishes or bolting.

Space: Grows well in garden beds, raised beds, or shallow containers (6–8 inches/15–20 cm deep).

Preparation

Soil: Loose, well-draining soil, rich in organic matter, with pH 6–7.

Pot/Vessel: Use a container with at least 6 inches (15 cm) depth.

Initial Fertilization: Incorporate compost or a balanced organic fertilizer before planting.

Planting

Timing:

Spring: Direct sow 4–6 weeks before the last frost, when soil temperature is at least 50°F (10°C).

Fall: Sow seeds 6–8 weeks before the first frost.

For continuous harvest: Sow every 7–14 days.

Method:

From Seeds: Sow seeds 1/4–1/2 inch (0.6–1.2 cm) deep and 1 inch (2.5 cm) apart in rows spaced 6–12 inches (15–30 cm) apart.

Thin seedlings to 2 inches (5 cm) apart once they emerge.

Germination: Seeds germinate in 3–10 days at 50–85°F (10–29°C).

Daily Care

Watering: Keep soil consistently moist but not waterlogged; water deeply 1–2 times per week to prevent splitting.

Fertilizing: Minimal fertilizing is needed; over-fertilization can lead to excessive leafy growth at the expense of roots.

Thinning: Thin seedlings to avoid overcrowding, ensuring roots have space to develop.

Pest and Disease Management

Pest and Disease Management

Common Issues:

Pests: Flea beetles, aphids, and root maggots.

Diseases: Downy mildew or damping off in wet conditions.

Solutions:

Use row covers to protect from pests.

Ensure good soil drainage and avoid overwatering to reduce fungal diseases.

Harvesting

When: Ready to harvest 20–30 days after planting, depending on the variety.

How:

Harvest when roots are 1–2 inches (2.5–5 cm) in diameter for the best flavor.

Pull gently from the soil or use a trowel to loosen roots.

Avoid leaving radishes in the ground too long, as they may become woody or split.

Practical Tips

Companion Planting: Grows well with carrots, lettuce, and beans. Avoid planting near brassicas like broccoli or cabbage.

Succession Planting: Sow small batches every 1–2 weeks for a continuous harvest.

Interplanting: Radishes grow quickly and can be planted among slower-growing crops like tomatoes or cucumbers.

Curiosities:

Radishes originated in Southeast Asia and were one of the first vegetables cultivated in Europe. They are rich in vitamin C and known for their detoxifying properties.

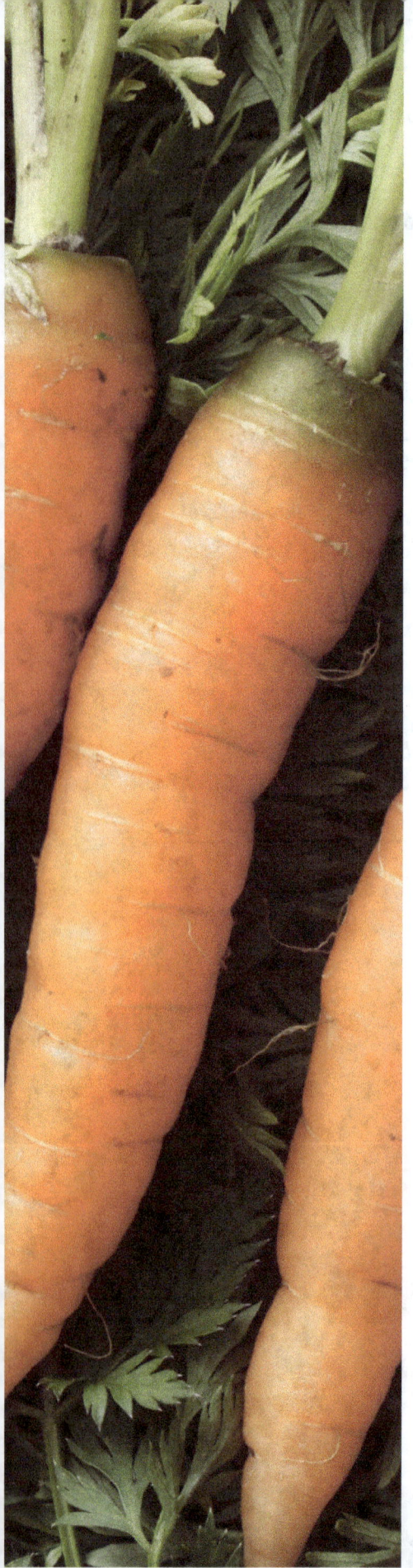

Baby Carrot

Baby carrots are a smaller, sweeter variety of carrots, ideal for snacking, salads, and cooking. They grow quickly and thrive in small spaces

Difficulty Level: Easy to moderate, requiring loose soil and consistent care.

Characteristics

Life Cycle: Biennial (commonly grown as an annual).

Size: Roots typically grow 2–4 inches (5–10 cm) long, with tops reaching 12 inches (30 cm).

Ideal Conditions

Light: Full sun to partial shade.

Climate: Prefers cool weather, 55–75°F (13–24°C). Warmer temperatures may cause bitterness.

Space: Grows well in raised beds or containers with a depth of at least 8 inches (20 cm).

Preparation

Soil: Loose, sandy, well-draining soil free of rocks, with pH 6–7.5. Deep, loose soil is critical to allow roots to grow straight.

Pot/Vessel: Use a container with at least 8–12 inches (20–30 cm) depth.

Initial Fertilization: Avoid excessive nitrogen; use compost or a fertilizer rich in phosphorus and potassium.

Planting

Timing:

Spring: Sow seeds 2–3 weeks before the last frost date when soil temperature is at least 50°F (10°C).

Fall: Sow seeds 10–12 weeks before the first expected frost.

Method:

From Seeds: Sow seeds 1/4 inch (0.6 cm) deep, spaced 1 inch (2.5 cm) apart in rows 8–12 inches (20–30 cm) apart.

Thin seedlings to 1–2 inches (2.5–5 cm) apart once they are 2 inches (5 cm) tall.

Germination: Seeds germinate in 7–21 days, depending on soil temperature and conditions.

Daily Care

Watering: Keep soil consistently moist but not waterlogged. Water deeply 1–2 times per week to encourage deep root growth.

Fertilizing:

Avoid high-nitrogen fertilizers to prevent excessive foliage growth over root development.

Use a balanced fertilizer or compost tea every 3–4 weeks.

Mulching: Use a light layer of mulch to retain soil moisture and keep the soil cool.

Pest and Disease Management

Common Issues:

Pests: Carrot rust flies, aphids, and cutworms.

Diseases: Root rot in overly wet conditions.

Solutions:

Use floating row covers to prevent pest infestations.

Avoid overwatering and rotate crops annually to minimize disease risks.

Harvesting

When: Ready to harvest 50–70 days after planting, depending on the variety.

How:

Gently pull carrots when they are 2–4 inches (5–10 cm) long and the tops are about 1/2 inch (1.3 cm) in diameter.

Loosen soil with a trowel if necessary to avoid breaking the roots.

Practical Tips

Succession Planting: Sow seeds every 2–3 weeks for a continuous harvest throughout the growing season.

Companion Planting: Grows well with onions, lettuce, and tomatoes. Avoid planting near dill or parsnips.

Thinning: Thin seedlings early to prevent overcrowding and ensure straight roots.

Curiosities:

Baby carrots were originally a solution for imperfect full-size carrots and became a popular snack due to their convenience and sweetness.

Beets

Beets are root vegetables with edible roots and leaves, valued for their sweet, earthy flavor and vibrant color. They are versatile in cooking and easy to grow.

Difficulty Level: Easy, suitable for beginners.

Characteristics

Life Cycle: Biennial (grown as an annual for roots).

Size: Roots grow 1–4 inches (2.5–10 cm) in diameter, with leafy tops reaching 12–18 inches (30–45 cm).

Ideal Conditions

Light: Full sun to partial shade.

Climate: Thrives in cool weather, 50–70°F (10–21°C). Heat can cause smaller roots and bolting.

Space: Suitable for garden beds, raised beds, or containers (minimum 12 inches/30 cm deep).

Preparation

Soil: Loose, fertile, well-draining soil with pH 6–7. Remove rocks to prevent misshapen roots.

Pot/Vessel: Use a container with a depth of at least 10–12 inches (25–30 cm).

Initial Fertilization: Enrich soil with compost or a low-nitrogen fertilizer high in phosphorus and potassium.

Planting

Timing:

Spring: Sow seeds directly outdoors 2–4 weeks before the last frost.

Fall: Plant 6–8 weeks before the first expected frost for a fall harvest.

Succession Planting: Sow seeds every 2–3 weeks for a continuous harvest.

Method:

From Seeds: Soak seeds in water for 24 hours before planting to speed up germination.

Sow seeds 1/2 inch (1.3 cm) deep and 1 inch (2.5 cm) apart in rows 12–18 inches (30–45 cm) apart.

Thin seedlings to 3–4 inches (7.5–10 cm) apart when they are 2–3 inches (5–7.5 cm) tall.

Germination: Seeds germinate in 5–12 days at 50–85°F (10–29°C).

Daily Care

Watering: Keep soil consistently moist but not waterlogged. Beets need about 1 inch (2.5 cm) of water per week.

Fertilizing:

Use a low-nitrogen fertilizer every 4–6 weeks to promote root growth.

Avoid excessive nitrogen to prevent overgrown tops and underdeveloped roots.

Mulching: Apply a thin layer of mulch to retain soil moisture and suppress weeds.

Pest and Disease Management

Common Issues:

Pests: Aphids, flea beetles, and leaf miners.

Diseases: Cercospora leaf spot and downy mildew.

Solutions:

Use neem oil or insecticidal soap for pests.

Ensure proper spacing and airflow to prevent fungal diseases. Rotate crops annually.

Harvesting

When:

Ready to harvest 50–70 days after planting, depending on the variety.

Baby Beets: Harvest when roots are 1–2 inches (2.5–5 cm) in diameter.

Full-Size Beets: Harvest when roots are 3–4 inches (7.5–10 cm) in diameter.

How:

Gently pull roots from the soil. Use a trowel to loosen the soil if necessary.

Harvest greens when they are 4–6 inches (10–15 cm) tall.

Practical Tips

Companion Planting: Grows well with lettuce, onions, and cabbage. Avoid planting near pole beans or field mustard.

Succession Planting: Stagger planting for continuous harvests.

Soil Preparation: Ensure soil is loose and rock-free to produce evenly shaped roots.

Curiosities:

Beets have been cultivated for over 4,000 years and were initially grown for their greens. The root became a culinary staple much later.

Peas

Peas are cool-season legumes grown for their sweet pods and seeds, perfect for snacking, cooking, or freezing.

Difficulty Level: Easy to moderate, requiring cool weather and trellising for climbing varieties.

Characteristics

Life Cycle: Annual.

Types: Shelling (garden) peas, snow peas, and snap peas.

Size: Bush varieties grow 1–3 feet (30–90 cm) tall; climbing varieties grow 4–8 feet (1.2–2.4 m) tall.

Ideal Conditions

Light: Full sun to partial shade.

Climate: Thrives in cool weather, 55–70°F (13–21°C). Heat can reduce yields.

Space: Suitable for garden beds, raised beds, or large containers (12 inches/30 cm deep).

Preparation

Soil: Well-draining, fertile soil with pH 6–7. Enrich soil with compost or a low-nitrogen fertilizer, as peas fix their own nitrogen.

Pot/Vessel: Use a container with a depth of at least 10–12 inches (25–30 cm) for bush varieties.

Trellising: Provide a trellis, stakes, or netting for climbing varieties.

Planting

Timing:

Spring: Sow seeds 4–6 weeks before the last frost, when soil temperature is at least 40°F (4°C).

Fall: Plant 8–10 weeks before the first expected frost.

Method:

Sow seeds 1 inch (2.5 cm) deep and 2–3 inches (5–7.5 cm) apart in rows spaced 18–24 inches (45–60 cm) apart.

For climbing varieties, plant in double rows with a trellis between rows.

Germination: Seeds germinate in 7–14 days, depending on soil temperature.

Daily Care

Watering: Keep soil evenly moist but not waterlogged. Water deeply once a week, increasing frequency during dry spells.

Fertilizing:

Avoid high-nitrogen fertilizers, as peas fix nitrogen naturally.

Add compost or organic fertilizer mid-season if needed.

Mulching: Use a light mulch to retain soil moisture and keep roots cool.

Pest and Disease Management

Common Issues:

Pests: Aphids, pea weevils, and slugs.

Diseases: Powdery mildew and root rot.

Solutions:

Use neem oil or insecticidal soap for pests.

Rotate crops annually to prevent diseases and improve soil health. Ensure good airflow around plants.

Harvesting

When:

Shelling Peas: Harvest 60–70 days after planting when pods are full and firm.

Snap Peas: Pick when pods are plump but tender.

Snow Peas: Harvest when pods are flat and seeds are just beginning to develop.

How:

Use scissors or pinch pods off the vine to avoid damaging the plant.

Check plants daily during peak harvest periods.

Practical Tips

Companion Planting: Grows well with carrots, radishes, and lettuce. Avoid planting near onions or garlic.

Succession Planting: Plant every 2–3 weeks for continuous harvests.

Trellising: Use stakes, twine, or netting to support climbing varieties and improve airflow.

Curiosities:

Peas were one of the first cultivated crops in human history, grown over 10,000 years ago. They are rich in protein, vitamins, and fiber.

.

Green Beans

Green beans, also called string beans or snap beans, are versatile, fast-growing legumes enjoyed fresh, steamed, or sautéed

Difficulty Level: Easy to grow, suitable for beginners.

Characteristics

Life Cycle: Annual.

Types: Bush beans (compact, do not need support) and pole beans (climbing, require trellising).

Size:

Bush beans: 12–24 inches (30–60 cm) tall.

Pole beans: Climb 6–10 feet (1.8–3 m) with support.

Ideal Conditions

Light: Full sun (6–8 hours daily).

Climate: Warm weather, 65–85°F (18–29°C). Sensitive to frost.

Space: Suitable for garden beds, raised beds, or containers (at least 12 inches/30 cm deep).

Preparation

Soil: Loose, well-draining soil, rich in organic matter, with pH 6–7.

Pot/Vessel: Minimum depth of 12–18 inches (30–45 cm), especially for pole beans.

Initial Fertilization: Enrich soil with compost or a low-nitrogen fertilizer.

Planting

Timing:

Spring: Sow seeds directly outdoors 1–2 weeks after the last frost when soil temperature is at least 60°F (16°C).

Succession Planting: Sow every 2–3 weeks for continuous harvests.

Method:

Bush Beans: Sow seeds 1 inch (2.5 cm) deep, spacing 2–3 inches (5–7.5 cm) apart in rows 18–24 inches (45–60 cm) apart.

Pole Beans: Sow seeds 1 inch (2.5 cm) deep, spacing 3–4 inches (7.5–10 cm) apart in rows 24–36 inches (60–90 cm) apart, providing a trellis or support.

Germination: Seeds germinate in 7–10 days at 65–85°F (18–29°C).

Daily Care

Watering: Keep soil evenly moist but not waterlogged. Water deeply once or twice a week, depending on weather.

Fertilizing:

Use a low-nitrogen fertilizer (e.g., 5-10-10) every 4–6 weeks to promote flowering and pod development.

Avoid excess nitrogen, as it encourages leafy growth over pods.

Support:

Pole beans: Use a trellis, stakes, or bean teepee for climbing varieties.

Bush beans: No support is needed.

Weeding: Keep the area weed-free, as weeds compete for nutrients and moisture.

Pest and Disease Management

Common Issues:

Pests: Aphids, spider mites, and bean beetles.

Diseases: Powdery mildew and bacterial blight.

Solutions:

Use neem oil or insecticidal soap for pest control.

Ensure proper spacing and crop rotation to reduce fungal and bacterial diseases.

Harvesting

When: Ready to harvest 50–70 days after planting, depending on the variety.

How:

Pick beans when they are 4–6 inches (10–15 cm) long and tender before seeds inside the pods swell.

Use scissors or pinch beans off the plant to avoid damaging vines.

Harvest every 2–3 days to encourage continued production.

Practical Tips

Companion Planting: Grows well with corn, squash, and carrots. Avoid planting near onions, garlic, or fennel.

Succession Planting: Sow new seeds every 2–3 weeks for extended harvests.

Pole Beans: Save space by growing vertically on a trellis or teepee.

Curiosities:

Green beans are native to Central and South America and have been cultivated for over 7,000 years. They are a rich source of fiber, vitamins, and protein.

Strawberries

Strawberries are sweet, juicy fruits that grow on compact plants and are popular in desserts, preserves, and fresh eating.

Difficulty Level: Easy to moderate, with proper planting and care.

Characteristics

Life Cycle: Perennial (best productivity during the first 2–3 years).

Types:

June-bearing: Produce one large crop in early summer.

Everbearing: Produce two crops (spring and fall).

Day-neutral: Produce smaller, continuous harvests throughout the growing season.

Size: Plants grow 6–12 inches (15–30 cm) tall and spread via runners.

Ideal Conditions

Light: Full sun (6–8 hours daily).

Climate: Thrives in mild, temperate climates, with temperatures between 60–80°F (15–27°C).

Space: Suitable for garden beds, containers, or hanging baskets.

Preparation

Soil: Rich, well-draining soil with pH 5.5–6.8.

Pot/Vessel: Use a container at least 6–8 inches (15–20 cm) deep, with good drainage.

Initial Fertilization: Incorporate compost or a balanced fertilizer before planting.

Planting

Timing:

Spring: Plant as soon as the soil is workable, after the danger of frost has passed.

Fall: In warmer climates, plant in late summer or early fall for an early harvest the following year.

Method:

Bare-root Plants: Space 12–18 inches (30–45 cm) apart in rows 2–3 feet (60–90 cm) apart. Plant so that the crown (where leaves meet roots) is just above the soil surface.

Container Planting: Plant one plant per 6–8 inch (15–20 cm) pot or space evenly in larger containers.

Runners: Remove runners during the first year to encourage root development.

Daily Care

Watering: Water deeply 1–2 times per week to keep the soil consistently moist but not waterlogged.

Fertilizing:

Use a balanced fertilizer every 4–6 weeks during the growing season.

Switch to a high-potassium fertilizer (e.g., 5-10-10) during flowering and fruiting stages.

Mulching: Add a layer of straw or pine needles to suppress weeds, retain moisture, and protect fruit from soil contact.

Pest and Disease Management

Common Issues:

Pests: Slugs, aphids, and birds.

Diseases: Powdery mildew, gray mold, and root rot.

Solutions:

Use neem oil or insecticidal soap for pests. Protect fruit from birds with netting.

Ensure good airflow and avoid wetting the foliage to prevent fungal diseases.

Harvesting

When: Begin harvesting 4–6 weeks after flowering.

How:

Pick strawberries when they are fully red and firm for maximum sweetness.

Gently twist or cut the stem just above the berry to avoid damaging the plant.

Harvest every 2–3 days during peak production.

Practical Tips

Companion Planting: Grow with lettuce, spinach, or borage. Avoid planting near brassicas or potatoes.

Runners: Remove runners to focus energy on fruit production, or use them to propagate new plants.

Winter Care: In colder climates, mulch heavily or cover plants with straw or frost blankets to protect them during winter.

Curiosities:

Strawberries are not true berries but aggregate fruits, developed from multiple ovaries. They are rich in vitamin C and antioxidants.

Swiss Chard

Swiss chard is a nutritious, leafy green with colorful stems, used in salads, sautés, and soups. It's easy to grow and highly productive

Difficulty Level: Easy, ideal for beginners.

Characteristics

Life Cycle: Biennial (commonly grown as an annual).

Size: Plants grow 12–24 inches (30–60 cm) tall.

Ideal Conditions

Light: Full sun to partial shade.

Climate: Thrives in cool to moderate temperatures, 50–75°F (10–24°C). Heat-tolerant but may become bitter in extreme heat.

Space: Suitable for garden beds, raised beds, or containers (minimum 10–12 inches/25–30 cm deep).

Preparation

Soil: Rich, well-draining soil with pH 6–7. Add compost or organic matter before planting.

Pot/Vessel: Use a container at least 10 inches (25 cm) deep, with good drainage.

Initial Fertilization: Mix a balanced fertilizer or compost into the soil before planting.

Planting

Timing:

Spring: Sow seeds 2–4 weeks before the last frost when soil temperatures are at least 50°F (10°C).

Fall: In warmer climates, plant 6–8 weeks before the first frost for a fall or winter harvest.

Method:

From Seeds: Sow seeds 1/2 inch (1.2 cm) deep and 2–4 inches (5–10 cm) apart in rows spaced 12–18 inches (30–45 cm) apart.

From Transplants: Plant seedlings 12 inches (30 cm) apart.

Thin seedlings to 6–12 inches (15–30 cm) once they reach 2–3 inches (5–7.5 cm) tall.

Germination: Seeds germinate in 5–10 days at 50–85°F (10–29°C).

Daily Care

Watering: Keep soil evenly moist but not waterlogged. Water deeply 1–2 times per week, especially in hot weather.

Fertilizing:

Apply a balanced fertilizer (e.g., 10-10-10) every 4–6 weeks to encourage leaf growth.

Use compost tea or liquid fertilizer mid-season for a boost.

Mulching: Mulch around plants to retain moisture and suppress weeds.

Pest and Disease Management

Common Issues:

Pests: Aphids, leaf miners, and slugs.

Diseases: Cercospora leaf spot and downy mildew.

Solutions:

Use neem oil or insecticidal soap for pests.

Ensure good airflow and avoid overhead watering to reduce fungal diseases.

Harvesting

When: Begin harvesting 30–60 days after planting, depending on the variety.

How:

Harvest outer leaves first, leaving the inner ones to continue growing.

Cut leaves at the base when they are 6–12 inches (15–30 cm) long.

For baby greens, harvest when leaves are 2–3 inches (5–7.5 cm) long.

Practical Tips

When: Begin harvesting 30–60 days after planting, depending on the variety.

How:

Harvest outer leaves first, leaving the inner ones to continue growing.

Cut leaves at the base when they are 6–12 inches (15–30 cm) long.

For baby greens, harvest when leaves are 2–3 inches (5–7.5 cm) long.

Curiosities:

Swiss chard is not native to Switzerland; it originates from the Mediterranean region. It is rich in vitamins A, C, and K, as well as minerals like magnesium and potassium.

Bok Choy

Bok choy, also known as pak choi or Chinese cabbage, is a fast-growing leafy vegetable with tender stalks and a mild, slightly sweet flavor. It's perfect for stir-fries, soups, and salads.

Difficulty Level: Easy to grow with proper care.

Characteristics

Life Cycle: Annual.

Size: Grows 6–24 inches (15–60 cm) tall, depending on the variety.

Ideal Conditions

Light: Full sun to partial shade; prefers partial shade in hotter climates.

Climate: Thrives in cool weather, 50–70°F (10–21°C). Heat may cause bolting.

Space: Grows well in garden beds, raised beds, or containers (minimum 8 inches/20 cm deep).

Preparation

Soil: Rich, well-draining soil with pH 6–7. Enrich with compost or organic matter.

Pot/Vessel: Use a container with at least 8–10 inches (20–25 cm) depth.

Initial Fertilization: Mix compost or a balanced fertilizer into the soil before planting.

Planting

Timing:

Spring: Sow seeds 2–4 weeks before the last frost.

Fall: Sow seeds 6–8 weeks before the first frost for a fall harvest.

Method:

From Seeds: Sow seeds 1/4–1/2 inch (0.6–1.2 cm) deep, spacing 6–8 inches (15–20 cm) apart for mature plants, or 2–4 inches (5–10 cm) apart for baby bok choy.

From Transplants: Space seedlings 6–12 inches (15–30 cm) apart.

Germination: Seeds germinate in 5–10 days at 50–75°F (10–24°C)

Daily Care

Watering: Keep soil consistently moist but not waterlogged. Bok choy prefers 1–1.5 inches (2.5–4 cm) of water per week.

Fertilizing:

Use a balanced fertilizer (e.g., 10-10-10) every 3–4 weeks.

Apply compost tea or liquid fertilizer during rapid growth phases.

Mulching: Add mulch to retain soil moisture and keep roots cool.

Pest and Disease Management

Common Issues:

Pests: Flea beetles, aphids, and cabbage worms.

Diseases: Downy mildew and clubroot.

Solutions:

Use row covers to protect young plants from pests.

Rotate crops annually to prevent diseases and improve soil health.

Harvesting

When:

Baby Bok Choy: Harvest 30–40 days after planting.

Full-Size Bok Choy: Ready in 45–60 days, depending on the variety.

How:

For baby leaves, snip individual leaves when 3–4 inches (7.5–10 cm) long.

For full heads, cut the plant at the base using a sharp knife.

Harvest before the plant bolts (produces flowers) for the best flavor.

Practical Tips

Companion Planting: Grows well with carrots, onions, and dill. Avoid planting near tomatoes or peppers.

Succession Planting: Sow seeds every 2–3 weeks for a continuous harvest.

Shade: Use shade cloth or plant in partial shade during warm weather to prevent bolting.

Curiosities:

Bok choy has been cultivated in China for over 1,500 years and is valued for its high vitamin A, C, and calcium content.

Daily Care and Maintenance

Watering Schedules: How Much Is Enough?

Watering is one of the most essential tasks in gardening, yet getting it right can sometimes be tricky. The key is finding the balance—too much water can drown your plants, while too little can leave them parched and stressed. Understanding how much is enough depends on your plants, soil type, and weather conditions.

Understanding Plant Needs

Different plants have varying water requirements. Vegetables like tomatoes, cucumbers, and peppers thrive in consistently moist soil, while drought-tolerant plants like herbs and succulents prefer drier conditions. Young seedlings and newly transplanted plants often need more frequent watering until their roots establish.

The best way to determine if your plants need water is to check the soil. Insert your finger about an inch (2.5 cm) into the soil. If it feels dry, it's time to water. For container plants, you may need to water more frequently, as pots tend to dry out faster than garden beds.

General Guidelines

Here is the information formatted into a table:

Watering Practice	Description
Early Morning Watering	Watering in the early morning allows plants to absorb moisture before the heat of the day causes evaporation. It also reduces the risk of diseases caused by wet foliage at night.
Water Deeply, Not Frequently	Deep watering a few times a week encourages roots to grow deeper into the soil, making plants more resilient during dry periods. Avoid light daily watering.
Adjust for Weather	Increase watering during hot, dry spells. Reduce watering during rainy periods to prevent over-saturation and waterlogging.

Soil and Watering

The type of soil in your garden plays a significant role in how often you should water. Sandy soils drain quickly, requiring more frequent watering, while clay soils retain moisture longer but can lead to waterlogging if overwatered. Amending soil with organic matter helps improve its ability to retain and drain water efficiently.

Signs of Overwatering and Underwatering

It's important to recognize the signs that indicate you may need to adjust your watering schedule:

Overwatering: Yellowing leaves, wilting despite wet soil, or signs of root rot. Underwatering: Drooping leaves, dry soil, or slow growth.

Container Gardening

For plants in containers, keep a close eye on moisture levels, as pots dry out faster than garden soil. Containers with proper drainage are essential to prevent waterlogging. During hot days, you may need to water container plants daily, especially if they are in direct sunlight.

Seasonal Adjustments

Watering needs change with the seasons. In spring and fall, when temperatures are cooler, plants require less water. In summer, especially during heatwaves, you'll need to water more frequently. Winter watering is minimal, except for overwintering crops or indoor plants.

By observing your plants and tailoring your watering routine to their needs, you can ensure healthy growth without wasting water. A well-hydrated garden is a thriving garden!

Fertilizing Basics: Natural vs. Synthetic Options

Fertilizers play a critical role in gardening by providing essential nutrients that plants need to grow and thrive. Choosing between natural and synthetic fertilizers depends on your gardening goals, preferences, and the specific needs of your plants. Here's a breakdown of both options to help you make an informed decision.

Type	Description	Advantages	Disadvantages
Natural Fertilizers	Derived from organic sources such as compost, manure, bone meal, and seaweed. They improve soil health over time.	- Improve soil structure and increase microbial activity. - Slow release of nutrients for sustained feeding. - Eco-friendly and sustainable.	- Slower to act compared to synthetic fertilizers. - Nutrient content can vary. - May require larger quantities.
Synthetic Fertilizers	Manufactured chemically to provide precise amounts of nutrients like nitrogen, phosphorus, and potassium (NPK).	- Quick and effective results. - Precise nutrient balance tailored to specific plants. - Easy to apply and widely available.	- Can lead to nutrient runoff and environmental damage. - May harm beneficial soil organisms. - Requires careful handling to avoid over-fertilizing.

When to Use Each

Natural Fertilizers: Best for long-term soil health and organic gardening. Ideal for preparing garden beds before planting and maintaining soil fertility over time.

Synthetic Fertilizers: Suitable for quick nutrient boosts, especially for plants showing immediate signs of nutrient deficiency. Useful in controlled environments like container gardening.

By understanding the pros and cons of each option, you can choose the fertilizer that aligns with your gardening style and sustainability goals while ensuring your plants get the nutrients they need.

Managing Common Pests and Diseases (Natural Remedies)

Gardening often comes with its challenges, including pests and diseases that can harm plants and reduce yields. However, with natural remedies, you can manage these issues effectively while keeping your garden eco-friendly and safe for pollinators, pets, and people. Here are some common pests and diseases and their natural management solutions:

Pest/Disease	Symptoms	Natural Remedies
Aphids	Clusters of small green, black, or white insects on leaves and stems; sticky residue on plants.	- Spray with a mix of water and a few drops of dish soap. - Introduce beneficial insects like ladybugs. - Use neem oil as a natural insecticide.
Slugs and Snails	Large irregular holes in leaves, trails of slime on soil and plants.	- Handpick at dawn or dusk. - Set traps with bowls of beer or create barriers with crushed eggshells or diatomaceous earth.
Caterpillars	Chewed leaves and visible larvae on plants.	- Remove caterpillars by hand. - Spray with Bacillus thuringiensis (Bt), a natural bacteria safe for plants.
Powdery Mildew	White, powdery spots on leaves and stems.	- Mix 1 teaspoon of baking soda with 1 quart (1 liter) of water and a drop of dish soap, then spray affected areas.
Blight (Tomatoes, Potatoes)	Brown spots on leaves and stems; wilting and yellowing of foliage.	- Remove infected plant parts. - Avoid overhead watering and ensure good air circulation. - Apply a copper-based fungicide sparingly.
Spider Mites	Tiny webbing on leaves, yellow or brown speckles on foliage.	- Spray plants with a strong stream of water to dislodge mites. - Use neem oil or insecticidal soap.
Whiteflies	Small white insects that fly when plants are disturbed; sticky residue on leaves.	- Use yellow sticky traps to catch adults. - Spray undersides of leaves with neem oil or insecticidal soap.
Cabbage Worms	Holes in cabbage, broccoli, or kale leaves; visible green worms.	- Sprinkle plants with food-grade diatomaceous earth. - Attract natural predators like birds.
Rust (Fungal Disease)	Orange or brown spots on leaves, especially on the underside.	- Remove and destroy infected leaves. - Use a sulfur-based fungicide or spray with a solution of baking soda and water.

General Prevention Tips

1. **Encourage Biodiversity**: Attract beneficial insects and birds to your garden by planting flowers like marigolds, daisies, and dill.
2. **Crop Rotation:** Avoid planting the same crops in the same location every year to disrupt pest and disease cycles.
3. **Healthy Soil:** Enrich your soil with compost and organic matter to support plant health, making them more resistant to pests and diseases.
4. **Proper Spacing:** Ensure good air circulation by avoiding overcrowding, which helps prevent fungal diseases.
5. **Mulching:** Use mulch to suppress weeds, retain soil moisture, and reduce pest habitats.

By addressing pest and disease problems naturally and preventatively, you can maintain a healthy, thriving garden without resorting to harmful chemicals.

Pruning and Supporting Plants for Better Growth

Pruning and providing proper support are essential practices for maintaining healthy plants, maximizing yields, and ensuring a tidy, well-organized garden. These techniques allow plants to focus their energy on growth, flowering, and fruiting while reducing the risk of disease and damage.

Pruning: Why It Matters

Pruning involves removing specific parts of a plant, such as dead, damaged, or overgrown branches, to promote healthier growth. It helps improve air circulation, sunlight penetration, and overall plant structure. Here are key pruning practices:

- Remove Dead or Diseased Parts: Regularly cut away dead or infected leaves, stems, or branches to prevent the spread of diseases and encourage new growth.

- Encourage Fruit Production: For fruiting plants like tomatoes and peppers, prune suckers (small shoots that grow between the main stem and branches) to direct energy to fruit-bearing branches.

- Shape and Control Growth: Pruning helps maintain the desired size and shape of plants, such as herbs, shrubs, or trees, while preventing overcrowding in your garden.
- Timing Matters: Prune most plants in late winter or early spring before new growth begins. For flowering plants, prune after blooming if they flower on old wood.

Supporting Plants

Some plants require physical support to grow upright, reduce stress on stems, and optimize space. Proper support systems also protect plants from wind damage and keep fruits and vegetables off the ground, minimizing pest and disease risks.

- **Staking:**
- Ideal for tall, single-stemmed plants like tomatoes, peppers, and sunflowers.
- Use wooden or metal stakes and tie stems gently with soft ties or fabric strips to avoid damage.

- **Trellising:**
- Best for vining plants like cucumbers, beans, and peas.
- Install a trellis or mesh netting for plants to climb, ensuring better air circulation and easier harvesting.

- **Caging:**
- Perfect for bushy plants like tomatoes, eggplants, or peppers.
- Tomato cages provide all-around support, helping plants maintain their shape and preventing branches from bending or breaking.

- **Netting and Strings:**
- Use for climbing plants like pole beans or gourds.
- Suspend lightweight netting or string between poles for plants to climb naturally.

Tips for Success

Use Clean Tools: Always use sharp, clean pruning shears or scissors to make precise cuts and reduce the risk of disease transmission.

Avoid Over-Pruning: Removing too much foliage can stress plants and reduce their ability to photosynthesize.

Secure Supports Early: Install supports at planting time or as early as possible to avoid disturbing root systems later.

Monitor Growth: Adjust ties and supports as plants grow to prevent girdling or constriction.

By integrating effective pruning and support techniques into your gardening routine, you'll enhance your plants' health and productivity, creating a thriving, efficient garden that's easier to manage.

Harvesting and Beyond

Recognizing When Vegetables Are Ready to Pick

Knowing when to harvest your vegetables is one of the most rewarding skills in gardening. Picking at the right time ensures the best flavor, texture, and nutritional value. While every vegetable has its own signals, there are general cues that can guide you in determining the perfect moment to harvest.

Vegetables often show their readiness through their size, color, and firmness. For example, a tomato's vibrant red hue and slight softness are signs it's ready to be picked, while cucumbers should be firm and evenly green. Observing the shape and growth pattern also provides valuable insight. Beans and peas, for instance, should be plump but not swollen, as overly mature pods can become tough and lose sweetness.

Touch is another reliable indicator. Root vegetables like carrots and radishes can be gently tugged from the soil to check their size. If they feel firm and have reached their expected diameter, they're ready. Similarly, leafy greens such as lettuce and spinach are best harvested when their leaves are tender and of medium size, avoiding overgrowth that can lead to bitterness.

Timing is also crucial, as vegetables often have specific windows of peak ripeness. Zucchinis, for instance, are most tender and flavorful when picked at about 6–8 inches (15–20 cm) long. Waiting too long may result in oversized, woody fruits. On the other hand, some crops, like kale or chard, allow for continuous harvesting of outer leaves while the plant continues to grow.

The seasons can provide additional clues, as certain vegetables, like pumpkins and winter squash, reach full maturity in late summer to early fall. These crops typically signal readiness when their skin hardens and their color deepens.

By observing your garden daily and paying attention to these natural cues, you'll gain a deeper connection to your plants and enjoy vegetables at their freshest and most delicious stage. Harvesting becomes a skill honed by experience, making it one of the most gratifying aspects of gardening.

How to Harvest Without Damaging the Plant

Harvesting vegetables is one of the most rewarding parts of gardening, but it's important to handle plants with care to ensure continued growth and productivity. With the right techniques, you can pick your crops without harming the plant or reducing its future yields.

When harvesting, always use clean, sharp tools such as scissors, pruners, or knives. This ensures a clean cut, reducing the risk of tearing stems or leaves, which can leave the plant vulnerable to pests and diseases. For delicate plants like lettuce or herbs, pinch or snip leaves near the base, avoiding the central growing point to encourage new growth.

For vegetables like tomatoes, peppers, and cucumbers, gently hold the fruit and twist it until it releases from the stem. Alternatively, use scissors or a knife to cut the fruit with a small portion of the stem attached, which can help prolong its freshness. Tugging or pulling roughly can damage the plant's branches or roots, potentially stunting its growth.

When harvesting leafy greens such as spinach or kale, focus on picking the outer, mature leaves first. This allows the plant to continue producing new leaves from the center. Similarly, for crops like zucchini or beans, harvest frequently to prevent overripe produce from weighing down or stressing the plant.

Root vegetables like carrots, radishes, or onions require a gentler approach. Loosen the soil around the base with a trowel or fork before pulling them out, ensuring their roots remain intact and reducing strain on the plant.

In fruiting plants or crops that produce continuously, like strawberries or basil, regular, small harvests encourage ongoing production. By removing only ripe fruits or leaves, the plant conserves its energy for future growth rather than repairing damage.

The key to harvesting without harming your plants lies in being observant, gentle, and methodical. Treat your plants with care, and they'll reward you with abundant, healthy produce throughout the growing season.

.

Storing Your Harvest: Fresh, Frozen, or Preserved

After putting in the effort to grow your vegetables, knowing how to store your harvest properly ensures you enjoy the fruits of your labor for as long as possible. Whether you plan to eat your vegetables fresh, freeze them for later, or preserve them through traditional methods, each option has its own benefits and techniques.

Storing Fresh

For the freshest flavor and texture, consume your vegetables soon after harvesting. Some crops, like leafy greens, cucumbers, and zucchini, are best stored in the refrigerator. Wrap them in a damp paper towel or place them in breathable bags to maintain their moisture without causing condensation. Root vegetables such as carrots, beets, and radishes can be stored for weeks if their tops are removed and they are kept in a cool, humid environment like a crisper drawer.

Hardier vegetables like onions, garlic, and winter squash do well in a dry, dark, and cool location. For potatoes, ensure they are stored in a dark place to prevent greening and bitterness, avoiding temperatures too cold to avoid converting their starches to sugar.

Freezing

Freezing is an excellent way to extend the life of your vegetables while retaining most of their nutrients. Many vegetables, such as beans, broccoli, and spinach, benefit from blanching before freezing. This process involves briefly boiling the vegetables and then plunging them into ice water to stop cooking, which helps maintain their color, texture, and flavor. Once blanched, dry the vegetables thoroughly and store them in airtight freezer bags or containers.

For herbs like basil, parsley, or cilantro, freezing in olive oil or water in ice cube trays is a convenient option for adding fresh flavor to future meals. Just pop out a cube and toss it into soups, sauces, or sautés.

Preserving

Preservation methods, such as canning, pickling, and drying, are time-honored techniques for storing your harvest long-term. Tomatoes can be canned as sauces or salsas, while cucumbers and other firm vegetables are ideal for pickling with vinegar, salt, and spices. Beets, peppers, and carrots are also excellent candidates for pickling.

Drying is a simple method for preserving herbs, chilies, and even certain fruits. Hang them in a well-ventilated, dark space or use a dehydrator to remove moisture, preserving their flavor and preventing spoilage.

For sweeter crops, like berries, jams and jellies are a classic way to preserve their flavor and enjoy them throughout the year.

Choosing the Right Method

The best storage method depends on the type of vegetable and how you plan to use it. While fresh storage works for short-term consumption, freezing and preserving allow you to enjoy your harvest well beyond the growing season. By combining methods, you can make the most of your garden's bounty, ensuring that none of your hard work goes to waste.

Expanding Your Garden

Companion Planting: What Grows Well Together

Companion planting is a gardening strategy where specific plants are grown together to promote healthy growth, deter pests, and improve yields. By understanding the natural relationships between plants, you can create a balanced, thriving garden that requires fewer chemical inputs and offers better productivity.

How Companion Planting Works

Some plants release natural chemicals that repel pests or attract beneficial insects, while others improve soil conditions or provide physical support for neighboring plants. Pairing these plants strategically not only saves space but also fosters a healthier garden ecosystem.

Here's a table outlining companion planting pairings for a thriving garden:

Plant	Companion Plants	Benefits
Tomatoes	Basil, marigolds, carrots, onions	Basil repels pests; marigolds deter nematodes; carrots loosen soil; onions deter aphids.
Carrots	Onions, leeks, rosemary, radishes	Onions and leeks repel carrot flies; radishes loosen soil; rosemary deters pests.
Cucumbers	Nasturtiums, dill, beans, sunflowers	Nasturtiums deter aphids; dill attracts beneficial insects; beans fix nitrogen; sunflowers provide shade.
Beans	Corn, squash, radishes, marigolds	Corn provides support; squash shades soil; marigolds repel beetles; radishes deter pests.
Corn	Beans, squash (Three Sisters), marigolds	Beans fix nitrogen; squash shades soil; marigolds repel pests.
Lettuce	Radishes, carrots, marigolds, strawberries	Radishes break up soil; marigolds deter nematodes; strawberries protect against aphids.
Peppers	Basil, onions, spinach, carrots	Basil deters aphids; onions repel pests; spinach and carrots maximize space efficiency.
Zucchini/Squash	Nasturtiums, beans, corn	Nasturtiums deter pests; beans fix nitrogen; corn provides support for climbing squash.
Potatoes	Beans, onions, marigolds	Beans fix nitrogen; onions repel pests; marigolds deter nematodes.
Strawberries	Borage, lettuce, spinach, onions	Borage attracts pollinators; lettuce and spinach provide ground cover; onions repel aphids.
Cabbage	Dill, onions, beets, nasturtiums	Dill attracts predatory insects; onions repel cabbage worms; nasturtiums deter aphids.

Vertical Gardening

Vertical Gardening for Small Spaces

Vertical gardening is an innovative and efficient solution for growing plants in small spaces. By taking advantage of vertical surfaces, you can maximize your gardening area while creating a visually appealing and productive space. This method works particularly well for urban environments, patios, balconies, or any area where horizontal space is limited.

Why Choose Vertical Gardening?

Vertical gardening allows you to grow more plants in less space by using walls, trellises, or hanging structures. It also improves accessibility, reduces bending for maintenance, and keeps plants off the ground, minimizing pest and disease risks. Additionally, vertical gardens can serve as decorative elements, transforming dull spaces into lush, green sanctuaries.

Best Plants for Vertical Gardening

Not all plants are suitable for vertical gardening, but many thrive in these conditions, especially those with trailing, climbing, or compact growth habits:

• Climbing Vegetables: Cucumbers, pole beans, peas, and tomatoes (with support).
• Compact Vegetables: Lettuce, spinach, and small pepper varieties.
• Herbs: Basil, parsley, mint, thyme, and chives.
• Fruits: Strawberries (in hanging pots) and compact berry bushes.
• Flowers: Nasturtiums, marigolds, and petunias, which also attract pollinators.

Techniques for Vertical Gardening

1. Trellises and Arches
Install trellises or arches for climbing plants like beans, peas, and cucumbers. As these plants grow upward, they make use of vertical space while keeping fruits and foliage off the ground.

2. Wall-Mounted Planters
Attach pots, pockets, or hanging baskets to walls or fences. These work well for compact vegetables, herbs, and flowers, creating a stunning green wall.

3. Hanging Gardens
Use hanging baskets or tiered planters to grow trailing plants like strawberries or herbs. Ensure that baskets have proper drainage and are securely fastened.

4. Pallet Gardens
Repurpose wooden pallets to create vertical growing spaces. Fill the slats with soil and grow shallow-rooted plants like lettuce, spinach, or herbs.

5. Tower Gardens
Use vertical planters or stackable containers to grow a variety of crops. These systems are perfect for small spaces and often come with built-in watering systems.

6. A-Frames or Ladders
Lean A-frame structures or ladders against walls to support pots or climbing plants. This simple setup allows for easy rearrangement and maintenance.

Care and Maintenance

Watering: Vertical gardens may dry out faster than traditional gardens due to their exposure. Use drip irrigation systems or water frequently to ensure plants stay hydrated.

Fertilizing: Regularly feed plants with liquid or slow-release fertilizers, as vertical setups may have less soil to hold nutrients.

Pruning and Harvesting: Prune plants regularly to prevent overcrowding and encourage healthy growth. Harvest frequently to maintain productivity.

Structural Stability: Ensure that all supports and containers are securely fastened to handle the weight of soil, plants, and water.

Vertical gardening is a creative and practical way to bring greenery into any space, no matter how small. With the right plants, structures, and care, you can enjoy a bountiful harvest and a beautiful garden, even in the tiniest of spaces.

Exploring Advanced Crops for Your Next Season

As your gardening skills grow, you might find yourself ready to move beyond beginner-friendly vegetables and herbs, venturing into advanced crops that offer unique challenges and rewards. These crops often require more attention, specialized care, or longer growing seasons, but they can elevate your garden to the next level in terms of variety and satisfaction.

What Are Advanced Crops?

Advanced crops are typically more demanding in terms of environmental conditions, space, or maintenance. They may require specific soil amendments, precise watering schedules, or protection from pests and diseases. However, the effort is well worth it, as these crops often produce exotic flavors, higher yields, or gourmet-quality produce.

Examples of Advanced Crops

Artichokes
Artichokes are a striking addition to any garden but require a long growing season and well-draining soil. These perennials thrive in mild climates and need regular fertilizing to produce large, tender buds.

Asparagus
Growing asparagus is an investment, as it takes 2–3 years to produce its first harvest. However, once established, it provides delicious spears each spring for 15–20 years. Asparagus thrives in rich, well-draining soil and benefits from consistent weeding and mulching.

Sweet Potatoes
Sweet potatoes need warm soil, plenty of space, and a long growing season to thrive. They are typically grown from slips (young shoots) rather than seeds, and their sprawling vines require room to spread or trellising in small spaces.

Melons (Cantaloupe, Watermelon)
Melons demand full sun, consistent warmth, and rich, well-draining soil. They require ample space for their sprawling vines and frequent watering during fruit development. Pollination is critical, so attracting bees is essential.

Cauliflower
Cauliflower can be temperamental, requiring cool temperatures and consistent watering to form firm, white heads. It's sensitive to heat and cold, making it important to time planting perfectly for spring or fall.

Brussels Sprouts
These slow-growing plants require a long growing season and cool weather to produce their best yields. Regular staking and pest management are essential for healthy sprout development.

Why Try Advanced Crops?

Enhanced Gardening Skills: Tackling these crops improves your understanding of soil management, pest control, and crop-specific techniques.

Unique Flavors: Advanced crops often provide gourmet-quality produce not commonly found in supermarkets.

Long-Term Rewards: Perennial crops like asparagus or artichokes offer a lasting harvest, rewarding your initial investment of time and effort.

By experimenting with advanced crops, you'll not only diversify your garden but also deepen your connection to the growing process. These challenges can lead to greater rewards, both in your harvest and in your development as a gardener. With preparation and care, your next season can be your most exciting yet!

Tips for Success

1. Start with One or Two Crops
Focus on one or two advanced crops to avoid feeling overwhelmed. This allows you to give them the attention they need while maintaining your existing garden.

2. Plan for Space and Time
Some crops, like melons and sweet potatoes, require significant room to spread, while others, like asparagus, need years to establish. Plan accordingly to make the most of your garden.

3. Prepare the Soil
Advanced crops often require rich, well-draining soil with specific nutrient needs. Test and amend your soil before planting to ensure optimal conditions.

4. Monitor Closely
Regularly check for signs of pests, diseases, or nutrient deficiencies, as these crops can be more susceptible to problems.

5. Use Companion Planting
Pair advanced crops with beneficial companions to deter pests, improve soil health, and maximize space.

Troubleshooting and FAQs

Common Problems and Solutions (Poor Growth, Pests, Overwatering)

Gardening is a rewarding endeavor, but it can sometimes come with challenges like poor growth, pest infestations, or overwatering. Understanding these common problems and their solutions can help you maintain a healthy, thriving garden.

Here's a table summarizing the common gardening problems and their solutions:

Problem	Cause	Solution
Poor Growth	Nutrient deficiency	Test soil and amend with compost or balanced fertilizer (e.g., 10-10-10). Tailor nutrients to plant needs, like nitrogen for leafy greens.
	Improper soil pH	Test soil pH and adjust with lime to raise pH or sulfur to lower it. Most plants thrive in a pH range of 6–7.
	Inadequate light	Relocate plants to ensure 6–8 hours of sunlight daily.
	Compacted soil	Loosen soil with a garden fork and add organic matter to improve aeration and drainage.
Pests	Aphids	Spray plants with water and dish soap, introduce ladybugs, or use neem oil.
	Caterpillars	Handpick off plants and apply Bacillus thuringiensis (Bt).
	Slugs and snails	Use beer traps, sprinkle diatomaceous earth, or handpick pests during early morning or late evening.
	Whiteflies	Use yellow sticky traps, spray neem oil, or rinse leaves with water.
Overwatering	Waterlogged soil	Water only when the top inch of soil feels dry. Ensure proper drainage in containers and garden beds.
	Root rot	Remove affected plants, improve drainage, and avoid overwatering.
	Inconsistent watering	Establish a regular watering schedule based on weather and soil conditions.

Tips for Overcoming Beginner Challenges

Challenge	Common Issue	Solution
Lack of Knowledge	Not knowing what to plant or when to plant.	Research plant profiles for your region. Start with beginner-friendly crops like lettuce, radishes, or herbs.
Limited Space	No access to large garden areas.	Use vertical gardening techniques, container gardening, or grow compact crops on balconies and windowsills.
Overwatering	Watering plants too frequently, causing root rot or stress.	Water only when the top inch of soil feels dry. Use containers with drainage holes and monitor soil moisture levels regularly.
Pests and Diseases	Plants damaged by aphids, caterpillars, or fungal infections.	Inspect plants regularly. Use natural remedies like neem oil, soap sprays, or companion planting to deter pests.
Poor Soil Quality	Soil lacks nutrients or has poor drainage.	Amend soil with compost or organic matter. Test pH levels and adjust to suit specific crops.
Time Constraints	Struggling to maintain regular care for the garden.	Start small with a few plants. Choose low-maintenance crops and set a consistent schedule for watering, weeding, and fertilizing.
Uneven Growth	Some plants thrive while others fail.	Group plants with similar light, water, and soil requirements. Ensure proper spacing for airflow and growth.
Weather Challenges	Extreme heat, frost, or unexpected rainfall damaging crops.	Use mulch to retain soil moisture, frost covers to protect plants, and raised beds to improve drainage during heavy rains.
Fear of Failure	Hesitation to start due to fear of making mistakes.	Accept that mistakes are part of learning. Begin with easy crops and celebrate small successes to build confidence.
Cost Concerns	Worry about the expense of setting up a garden.	Reuse containers, make your own compost, and swap seeds with friends. Start with affordable materials and expand gradually.

This table highlights common beginner challenges and practical solutions to overcome them, helping you build confidence and enjoy gardening.

When to Seek Help from Gardening Communities

Joining gardening communities can be an invaluable resource when you're facing challenges or simply looking to enrich your gardening experience. These groups are filled with individuals who have a wealth of knowledge, ranging from experienced horticulturists to fellow beginners eager to share their journeys. Knowing when to seek help from these communities can make all the difference in cultivating a successful garden.

One of the most common reasons to turn to gardening groups is when you encounter plant issues you can't identify. Perhaps your plants are showing unusual symptoms like discoloration, spots, or stunted growth, and you've tried all the usual remedies with no success. Gardening communities can help pinpoint the problem, whether it's a pest, disease, or nutrient deficiency, and provide practical, often region-specific solutions.

Another reason to reach out is when pests become a persistent problem. If aphids, slugs, or other nuisances have overrun your garden despite your best efforts, members of these groups can share advice on effective natural pest control methods, often based on their personal experiences in similar situations.

Soil and nutrient concerns are another area where these communities shine. If you're unsure about the quality of your soil or how to balance nutrients for a particular crop, seasoned gardeners can guide you through soil testing, amendments, and crop-specific feeding practices. Similarly, when you're unsure about planting schedules, frost dates, or what grows best in your climate, local gardening groups are an excellent resource. Their advice is tailored to your region, helping you make confident decisions about when and what to plant.

For those venturing into more advanced gardening projects, such as growing challenging crops like artichokes, asparagus, or melons, gardening communities offer targeted tips to help you succeed. They're also great when you're trying new techniques, such as vertical gardening or permaculture, as experienced members can share tutorials, workshops, and stories from their own attempts.

Beyond problem-solving, gardening groups provide inspiration and support. If you're feeling stuck or discouraged, they can reignite your enthusiasm with creative ideas, success stories, and encouragement. They're also wonderful for helping you deal with surplus harvests, whether through tips on preserving your produce, participating in seed or crop swaps, or even donating excess to community food programs.

Perhaps most importantly, gardening communities offer connection. They're a space to network with like-minded individuals, share your knowledge, and learn from others. Whether you're seeking advice, looking to join a community garden, or simply want to share your successes, these groups foster a sense of camaraderie that makes gardening even more rewarding.

By engaging with gardening communities, you open yourself up to a world of collective wisdom, support, and creativity that can enhance your gardening journey in countless ways.

Conclusion

Gardening is much more than planting seeds and harvesting crops—it's a journey of growth, learning, and connection. Whether you're cultivating vegetables for fresh, homegrown meals, experimenting with advanced crops, or transforming a small space into a lush vertical garden, the rewards extend far beyond the physical harvest.

Through the seasons, gardening teaches patience, resilience, and the importance of nurturing, not just in the soil but within ourselves. It fosters a deeper appreciation for nature's cycles and reminds us of the value of sustainable, mindful living. Even when challenges arise, such as pests, poor growth, or unpredictable weather, each obstacle becomes an opportunity to learn and adapt, making every success even more satisfying.

Gardening communities, with their wealth of shared knowledge and camaraderie, highlight the collaborative spirit of this timeless activity. They offer a place to seek help, share experiences, and celebrate achievements, turning gardening into more than a solitary pursuit—it becomes a shared passion that connects people.

No matter your experience level or the size of your garden, the act of growing something with your own hands is profoundly rewarding. From tiny balconies to sprawling backyards, every space has the potential to flourish. With the right tools, guidance, and determination, anyone can create a thriving garden that brings joy, sustenance, and beauty into their lives.

So dig in, plant that first seed, and watch how your efforts grow—not just in your garden, but in your understanding, confidence, and connection to the world around you. Gardening truly is a gift that keeps giving, season after season.

www.ingramcontent.com/pod-product-compliance
Lightning Source LLC
Chambersburg PA
CBHW081724120626
46550CB00010B/3243